Juliane M. Howard

Coming Home To Me

*"A journey of Inner Child Healing,
Faith, and Finding Wholeness"*

Published by Mindset Films™

First Edition
Printed in the United States of America
ISBN: 979-8-218-65481-8   Published
by Mindset Films™
www.mindsetfilms.com

The author is not a licensed therapist or counselor, and this book is
not intended as a substitute for professional mental health treatment.
Unless otherwise indicated, all scripture quotations are taken from
the Holy Bible, King James Version (KJV), which is in the public
domain.

Dedication

To my son, **Aaron Black** —
I want you to know just how deeply proud I am of you.
You are a strong, wonderful young man with so much to give this
world. I admire your resilience, your heart, and your ability to stand
strong through life's challenges.

You are wiser than I ever was at your age, and your compassion is
one of your greatest gifts.

Always remember how truly special you are.
Never stop caring for others — and never forget how much you are
loved.

With all my heart,
Mom

ACKNOWLEDGMENTS

A Fighter's Legacy
(To You Mom)

One thing I've come to truly understand is just how strong my mother is. After enduring a problematic surgery—one that left her with lasting health challenges and only a slim chance of recovery—she continued to defy the odds, day after day. My mom chose to live where others might have surrendered to their limitations. She faced pain and struggle but still did the everyday things. She kept showing up, even when it wasn't easy. She never threw in the towel. She was a fighter—not a quitter.

Growing up, I didn't always recognize the depth of her strength. But now, I do. I see how much quiet bravery she carried and how much it took for her to keep going. That same strength lives in me. Even when I feel like giving up, I remember—I come from a line of women who didn't quit.

Her fight looked different than mine, but in many ways, we were both battling to stay standing in the face of circumstances that could have broken us. I carry her resilience with me—not as a burden but as a gift. And that legacy has shaped who I am becoming. I am no longer just surviving. I am living. Becoming. Rising.

And for the first time, I believe I am enough—just as I am.

To my husband, Stan —

Thank you for standing beside me through the ups and downs. Your presence, love, and support have meant more than I can put into words.

To my family and friends —

Thank you for loving me through my becoming.
Your encouragement, prayers, and belief in me have helped carry this book to life.

To Lindsay Wagner —

Thank you for helping me see that those trap doors inside me could be opened.
Your insight and kindness helped me shift the way I view my past — and myself.
Because of you, I found the courage to walk toward healing with hope instead of fear.

With deep gratitude,
Juliane M. Howard

Table of Contents

Introduction

I never thought I would write a book like this. For most of my life, I kept my story quiet—either because I didn't know how to tell it, or because I believed no one wanted to hear it. I told myself my pain wasn't big enough, my trauma wasn't "bad enough," and my voice wasn't strong enough. But something inside me knew that healing had to start with truth. And truth begins when you're ready to stop hiding.

This book is not about blame. It's not about having all the answers. It's about discovering that no matter how broken you feel, there's still a path home. For me, that path began with my inner child—the parts of me that were still hurting, still believing the lies of the past, still waiting for someone to come back and say, "You matter. You've always mattered." When I finally opened my heart to those little girls inside me, everything changed. Slowly. Gently. Powerfully. And the truth is—this work is still unfolding every day. This book is the story of that process—of coming home to me after years of abandonment, rejection, shame, and silence. And even more than that… it's about coming home to the truth of who I am in Christ.

It's not perfect. This has been the hardest thing I've ever done. Being told what to do and how to do it would have been simple—but facing the pain head-on and allowing it to surface? That has been unreal. True healing never is easy. But it's real. And it's honest. And I hope it speaks to the part of you that's still waiting to be seen.

If you've ever felt unworthy, unseen, or alone… this book is for you. Not to give you all the answers, but to remind you that you are not the only one. And you are never too far gone.

God has never stopped loving you. And He is the One guiding you home.

With love and understanding,

Juliane M. Howard

Chapter 1 – The Soil I Was Planted In

I was born on January 16, 1968, a child of the '70s—an era when times were tough, and survival was the name of the game. Kids were expected to stay outside, use their imagination, and play until the streetlights came on. Time inside the house or in front of a TV was rare and often discouraged. Parents were strict. Discipline wasn't just common—it was expected. Today, spanking is controversial; back then, it was frowned upon if you didn't spank your child. Sticks, switches, belts—anything within reach—were considered fair game. And where on the body did they land? That didn't matter much.

My mother had endured a harsh life herself. At just 13 years old, she was diagnosed with a brain tumor. The surgery at that time only removed part of the tumor. Two years later, at age 15, she underwent a second surgery to remove the remaining portion of the tumor, which was very close to her brain. The aftermath was devastating—she had to relearn everything: how to walk, talk, eat, and function as a human being. Doctors gave grim predictions. But my mom was a fighter.

She came home in a wheelchair, and her five brothers refused to let her accept that fate. They got her out of the chair, helped her walk, and pushed her forward. Before long, she walked independently, defying everything the doctors had said she'd never do.

She went on to get her license as a professional hair stylist and even owned her own business. She married—though not wisely—and in 1968, she had me.

We lived with her mother, sister, and brother in a two-bedroom house—yes, a two-bedroom home for all of us. I remember when our first bathroom was finally installed. I shared a hideaway bed with my mother in the living room. My father was never part of my life. I never met him as a child, but I did meet him years later.

Christmas and birthdays were exciting! I got so many gifts. They had to put them in a separate bedroom just to make space. And the clothes I loved the most were the old hand-me-down bags from my mom's friend's kids. I would dig through them like buried treasure, trying on outfit after outfit, running around in them for a while, and changing again just minutes later. It felt like an extra Christmas every time.

Sure, I got new clothes too—but I didn't love those the same way. The surprise of those bags, the variety, the stories behind the pieces they meant more to me than anything fresh off a store rack. These days, some kids might roll their eyes at the idea of secondhand clothes and say, "Really? Someone else's stuff?"

But for me, I preferred it. It made me feel special. It made me feel remembered.

Not every memory from that time was heavy. One day, when I was maybe six or seven, my mom was learning how to drive. She had this little VW Bug, and I rode along while she practiced. I wasn't scared; I was having fun. I still remember giggling in the passenger seat, bouncing as she tried to figure out the clutch. It was one of the moments where life felt light. She was trying something new, and I got to be right there with her. Looking back now, I loved those moments and I clung to them.

I was an only child, raised as a tomboy. I lived outside, got dirty, took risks, and was as wild as any boy. But while my days were filled with activity, I suffered from emotional problems.

Many parents raise their children the way they were raised. And back then, survival came first. Emotions were luxuries. Mental health wasn't something people talked about. If you were struggling inside, the answer was usually: "Get over it."

My mother survived more than most. She showed strength, which I still admire to this day. However, even strength can come with scars, and sometimes, those scars affect how we love the next generation. Emotional needs weren't often recognized in our home—not because there wasn't love, but because there was survival.

In the post-World War II era, parenting was authoritarian—focused on control and discipline. Emotions were dismissed, and communication was one-way: "Because I said so." Physical health was prioritized, and mental well-being was rarely acknowledged.

There was a shift during the 1960s and '70s—some parents became more permissive, allowing warmth and self-expression. But even then, emotional needs were often overlooked, and children were left to self-regulate without the tools.

Mental health awareness was beginning to rise, but it was still heavily stigmatized. Most families didn't seek help unless something was visibly wrong. Depression in children was rarely diagnosed unless the symptoms were extreme. Anxiety was more commonly recognized but often mislabeled as stress or overreaction.

Even when help was sought, institutions weren't equipped to offer healing. Occupational therapy centers and hospitals often grouped patients together, regardless of their specific needs, and provided little proper support.

Society viewed mental health as something shameful. If you were struggling, the message was clear: "Pull yourself together." Therapy was rare. Vulnerability was a weakness.
And children like me—quietly hurting —had no voice.
This was the world I came into. This was the soil I was planted in.
And from that soil, I would grow—searching, aching, yearning for something I couldn't name: safety, connection, and love.

But it would take me decades to understand that what I was searching for... was me.

Reflection - Early Wounds, and Search for Healing When did I first realize something from my childhood still affected me today?

As A child, I had anxiety and panic attacks. It wasn't something that developed later in life—it was how I was wired from the beginning. I knew no different way of feeling until recently. For years, I thought that heaviness in my chest, that constant edge of fear, was just life. I didn't know there was another way to feel.

But now I do. And realizing that truth was the beginning of everything changing.

What messages—spoken or unspoken—did I receive about my worth as a child?

The loudest message I got—though no one would admit to sending it—was that my feelings didn't matter. I was a kid, which meant it was okay to laugh at me, tease me, and even ridicule me in front of adults—men and women alike. It was all fun and games, they thought. But it didn't feel fun to me. It didn't feel very comfortable. What no one seemed to realize is that children remember.

If something wounds you deeply enough, it stays.

The shame I felt was real.

The message was clear: I didn't matter.

Who did I look to for comfort when I was little? My grandma. She was a tough lady—always busy, always doing something—but she was wise. She used to say, "If you just sit a child down and talk to them, they'll listen." And she was right. She was soft-spoken, and I knew she cared. But even when she was holding me, I couldn't relax. My mind would race with so many "what ifs." Is my mom going to be home? Will she fall and hit her head again?

What if she dies while she's gone?

That kind of fear doesn't let go quickly. And when Grandma answered me with the truth—"If she dies, she'll be with God, but I hope it doesn't happen"—it wasn't enough. Not to a child. I needed guarantees. I needed security. And when you only have one parent, the fear of losing them is consuming.

I didn't know what to call it back then, but I was already learning how to suppress my needs and carry fear I couldn't explain. I was learning anxious attachment in the soil I was planted in.

Bonus Reflection: Uncovering Anxious Attachment

Growing up, I never thought of certain moments as emotional abuse. It wasn't meant that way — it came from care. But I've since learned that intention doesn't erase impact. Sometimes, the things said in love can still leave deep marks.

My grandmother once warned me to "watch out" for my mom —
saying that if she ever fell and hit her head, it could kill her.

At the time, I didn't understand what that did to my nervous system.
But looking back, I realize it changed everything.

How This Experience Could Fuel Anxious Attachment:

1. **Hypervigilance and Fear of Loss**
   I grew up afraid. Constantly scanning my world for danger. I
   believed I was responsible for keeping my mom alive. This
   kind of fear wires a child for anxiety — and as an adult, it
   shows up as fear of loved ones dying. I also learned that love
   could vanish and that made me cling tighter to people.

2. **Role Reversal (Parentification)**
   I became the caretaker as a child. The protector. And in
   doing that, I learned to ignore my own needs. My pain didn't
   matter — only keeping others safe did. That pattern followed
   me for years.

3. **Catastrophic Thinking**
   That warning wasn't just a sentence — it was a script that
   shaped how I thought. I expected loss. I expected
   abandonment. I braced for the worst in everything.

Signs This Affected Me as an Adult

- Reading too much into silence or small changes in tone
- Feeling unworthy or needing constant reassurance
- Becoming emotionally exhausted trying to hold relationships together
- Struggling to ask for my own needs to be met

How I've Started to Heal

- I've named the link. I now see how my childhood created these patterns.
- I've reparented myself. I've spoken truth to the little girl who was afraid.
- I'm setting boundaries. Slowly, gently, I'm learning that my needs matter too.
- I've sought help. Through practices like EFT, meditation, and even EMDR, I used 9 Gamut. I've started rewriting the script that trauma once wrote for me.

My grandmother's words were spoken in love. But they unintentionally left me with a survival-level burden.

Today, I choose to carry truth instead.
I am not responsible for keeping the world safe. I am responsible for learning how to feel safe in the world.

Chapter 1 – Bonus Journal Prompts *(Exploring childhood wounds, first emotional memories, and early beliefs)*

1. **What's one early memory that shaped how you see yourself today?**

Think about a moment from your childhood—positive or painful—that left a mark. What did it teach you about your worth?

About your voice?

About whether you were safe or valued?

What belief might you still carry from that moment?

2. **What would you go back and say to the younger you in that memory?**

If you could step into that exact moment now as the adult you are today, what would you say to the younger version of you?

What comfort, truth, or strength would you offer her?

Chapter 2 – The Unseen Girl

As a little girl, I stayed at home. We were made to be outside—it was our element. Coming inside was hardly ever an option unless the weather said otherwise. Even on snow days, I often went out underdressed and didn't feel a thing. My mom would bring me inside and bundle me up. I hated it because I had such a heavy outfit on I couldn't move. We were just kids being kids.

But not every day was filled with adventure or laughter.
From a young age, my grandmother told me, "Julie, watch out for your mom. If she falls and hits the back of her head, it could kill her." Those words hit hard for a small child. There was no explanation or follow-up to soften the fear. I took them as truth—deadly, urgent, and final. That warning embedded itself into my little spirit.

I couldn't leave her side. I was terrified that if she fell when I wasn't there, it wouldn't just hurt her—it would end her life.

So, when Mom started dating again as a single parent, I didn't want to go with her to be nosy or clingy. I wanted to go to protect her. When I wasn't allowed to go on dates with her, I stayed home with anxiety and panic in my heart. My mind raced, believing only the most horrific scenes that could happen. That horrible feeling of doom settled in my body like I was sitting in a hospital waiting room, dreading the surgeon's update. I truly believed that if I went to sleep, I would wake up and discover she had never come home.

That fear stayed with me. I remember it clearly as if it happened yesterday, and in some ways, it still lives in me today. But now, through my healing work, I meet that little girl with open arms. I call her my Inner Child. When the fear rises, I cradle her gently. I hold her close, warmly speak to her, and remind her she is safe.

Growing up, no one helped me understand or manage that fear. Instead, I remember comments like, "Don't be ridiculous," or "Well, if anything happens, mom will go to heaven."
I am sure those words brought comfort to the adults around me, but for a little girl under eight years old with no father, no siblings, and only her mother, they felt cold and uncaring. They didn't ease the fear and quiet the worry. In fact, they made it worse. It felt less like reassurance and more like quiet preparation for something tragic— like they were gently bracing me for the worst.

Many people who joke and tease don't realize how deeply those actions can hurt, especially with a child. My uncle loved me—I know that—but he also tormented me in ways he probably thought were simply playful.

He would laugh at me, make fun of me, and, without realizing it, make me feel ashamed.

That kind of teasing wasn't limited to just one person. I also experienced it from other family members. To them, it may have felt like harmless fun, but to me, it made me want to disappear. Their words and actions slowly grabbed my spirit, making me question myself. This taught me early on that something must be wrong with me. What felt like playful fun to them became, for me, an intense hatred for myself.

One moment that never left me was when a different uncle—someone who wasn't even around that often—looked at me one day, stuck out his tongue, and called me "fatty." I was stunned. Later, when I looked back at pictures of myself standing next to his daughter, I noticed something glaring; we were the exact same size, which was average. And she was never called fat. That moment planted a seed of shame in me—one I carried silently for years.

My mother loved me, I know that—but she was emotionally detached from me. It wasn't something she knew how to give. She had survived so much herself, and in many ways, she was still learning how to feel safe in the world. Looking back now, I realize that her parenting style wasn't just about her personal struggles—it was also shaped by the world she grew up in.

Sometimes, I needed comfort, connection, or someone to ask how I felt—but those things didn't happen. I was expected to be tough and move on. But the feelings I kept inside were the very things I needed help understanding. I needed to talk about them, to learn what they meant. Instead, I buried and dealt with them the only way I knew how—alone.

Looking back, maybe I could have sat down with my mom and tried to talk, but that never felt like an option. That kind of closeness just wasn't something we did.

As I grew older, the wounds from my early years began to shape how I saw myself—and how I interacted with the world around me. When I first started kindergarten, I didn't stay long. I lasted about six weeks before I was held back.

Every morning, my mom would take me to school, and every time she left, I cried—not just a little—all day. The teachers tried to comfort me, but nothing worked. I was terrified—not of school, but of what might happen if I wasn't there.

That fear had a particular root.
Remembering those words, my grandmother had warned me:
"Watch out for your mom. If she falls and hits her head, it could kill her."

I carried those words like a life-or-death responsibility.

As a little girl, I truly believed that my presence might be the thing keeping my mom alive. So, the idea of leaving her—even for a few hours—was more than I could handle. If something happened to her while I was away, it would be my fault for not being there.

Eventually, the decision was made to keep me home. And to be honest, I was relieved. I felt safe at home—not just because I was with her but because I believed my being there was keeping her safe, too. What I didn't know—what no one taught me—was that it was never supposed to be my job to protect my mother.

I learned my ABCs and numbers at home, but I wasn't socially ready when I first grade. I didn't know how to connect with the other kids. Most of the time, my mind was on my mom—wondering if she was okay and hoping nothing had happened to her while I was gone. That constant concern made it hard for me to develop friendships or feel present with kids my age.

I struggled to fit in. Kids teased me, and I often felt like an outcast. No one wanted to play with me. But one day, one of my classmates, a girl with special needs who was also often bullied and laughed at like me, started hanging out with me. I won't mention her name for her privacy, but I remember her with deep affection.

She and I had something in common: we were both outsiders. And somehow, in the quiet space of being rejected by others, we found comfort in each other.

One day during recess, we didn't go to the playground like we were supposed to. Instead, we wandered behind the building and started running between the office doors and the cafeteria. We weren't hurting anyone or breaking anything—we were playing. But when the school found out, I got into trouble. And when I got home, it only got worse.

What hurt the most wasn't the punishment. It was what came after. The school discouraged me from continuing my friendship with that little girl. They even told my mom they didn't think it was a good idea for us to socialize. I didn't understand it then, but I felt the sting of it—being told that the one person who accepted me wasn't someone I should be around.

It was a message that stayed with me far longer than it should have: Even the people who accept you aren't acceptable.

That moment was one of the first times I learned that fitting in didn't always mean feeling seen. Sometimes, it meant letting go of the people who did see you because they didn't fit the mold either.

Around the age of seven, something shifted. It was the first time I experienced what a real friendship could feel like. My mom started doing hair for a woman who came to our house every weekend, and she brought her young daughter with her. While our mothers were inside, we were outside running around, playing games, making up stories, and just being kids. We had our share of grand adventures. We played Charlie's Angels; she was always Jill Monroe, and I was Kelly Garrett. The Bionic Woman, well, we were both bionic. If they could do it, we believed we could too. That even meant jumping off the roof of my house. At eight years old, we somehow knew how to land without breaking every bone in our bodies. Looking back, we should have grown up to train stunt doubles.

We clicked so quickly. I didn't feel strange or out of place for the first time. I didn't have to work so hard to be liked. She just liked me. And that simple truth—someone choosing me just because they wanted to—was healing.

She became my childhood friend. We played every weekend. We laughed. We created our little world. And even though I still carried worry about my mom and struggled in other parts of life, those moments with her gave me something precious.

Even though I had my weekend friendships—those sweet moments of fun and laughter—I still had to face school five days a week, and school wasn't safe for me. To this day, my heart goes out to the people who are going through this type of abuse. I understand how it feels.

Words were said to me that never left. Words, reactions, and outright dismissals shaped how I saw myself. They taught me who I was allowed to be and who I wasn't. I began to believe what they told me, not because it was true, but because no one offered me a different story.

As a kid, you count on what others think about you too much. That's how it is—especially when you don't come out of the shoot grounded or put together. When no one has poured confidence or stability into you, you become a mirror for everyone else's opinions. And when those opinions are cruel, you carry them like facts.

As a little girl, I only had my family to turn to when things hurt. I didn't have teachers or peers to confide in. So, when I brought even a piece of my pain home—trying to talk about the teasing, the rejection, the ache—I was hoping for comfort, understanding, and a safe place to cry. Instead, my mom got angry.

Not at me, but at the situation. At the people who hurt me. She didn't like anyone talking bad about her kid, and she had lived through her version of the same pain even though she was dealing with different players.

Her advice was clear and sharp: "Tell them to kiss your ass and walk away." (And yes—she added even more colorful words, but I'll leave those to the imagination.) She wasn't being cruel. She was trying to protect me.

She wanted me to toughen up because she knew the world wasn't fair—and never would be. She didn't want me to be crushed by it like she had been. But I wasn't wired like her. I was emotionally needy, soft-hearted, searching for something gentle.

What I needed was a hug. What I needed was someone to say, "I'm sorry they hurt you. I know it hurts. You don't deserve that." But instead, I got a battle cry.

While I understand now that her anger came from love, it didn't feel that way back then. It felt like she was brushing off my pain, telling me to get over it, dismissing the thing that was breaking me inside. She wasn't. She didn't know how to give me the kind of love I needed.

And that misunderstanding—between her love and my longing—would shape how I tried to survive the world around me.

By the time I reached fourth grade, the weight of that hurt became even heavier. I was bullied and teased relentlessly, and my self-esteem, already fragile, felt almost nonexistent. I remember pretending to be sick in the mornings to avoid going to school. I hated that place with every fiber of my being.

It didn't help that I struggled academically. I was often placed in the lowest reading groups, and my spelling was consistently poor. Spelling still isn't my strength. I didn't just feel left behind in school — I truly couldn't keep up.

I had trouble reading and spelling. No matter how hard I tried, I couldn't pronounce unfamiliar words — even when teachers encouraged us to "sound them out." My brain just didn't seem to work that way. I'd reread the same paragraph or chapter repeatedly and still have no idea what I had just read. It was like the words were there... but they couldn't find a way in.

Spelling wasn't any easier. I couldn't break words down phonetically the way others did. I couldn't piece them together. Even words I had seen before felt foreign on the page.

And while others seemed to grow more confident in class, I only grew more ashamed. I didn't understand what was wrong with me — only that I was different. And in a world where school meant worth, I silently concluded what no child should ever have to: "Your Stupid."

That message burrowed in deep. And for decades, it would echo anytime I tried something new… anytime I opened my mouth… anytime I dreamed too loudly.

I was no longer just an outsider—I was the girl people laughed at. The one no one wanted to sit with. The one who felt like the worst kid in the world simply for existing.

One day in class, we sat quietly, looking at the board while the teacher spoke. I was paying attention, watching him write instructions on the board; I was listening, and then, out of nowhere, the teacher called out:
"Julie, what are you doing?" I
looked at him, curious.
"Nothing," I said honestly.
And he snapped back with,
"Exactly!"
The entire classroom laughed.
I felt heat generated throughout my body. Crawling under the desk would not have helped me overcome this laughter. I had no idea what I had done wrong, and I would not ask.

We weren't writing. We weren't doing anything but listening to instructions, and somehow, I had become the butt of this teacher's joke.

That moment crushed me.

It didn't just embarrass me—it shamed me. And it wasn't new. That same thick, awful feeling had poured over me before. This is the kind of shame that creeps into your body and makes you want to disappear.

That one comment, in front of everyone, confirmed the story I was already telling myself: Julie, you're stupid. You're no good. You're the reason for all this pain. The worst part about this bully? It came from someone I was supposed to trust—a teacher, an adult.

This was yet another layer of the armor I was already wearing. I am steadily being taught that I'm still wrong even when I try my best. It made me feel less than—like something was wrong with me. When you already feel invisible or not good enough, these small struggles start to feel like permanent proof that you don't measure up.

At one point, I even called another school district and begged the principal to let me transfer. I asked what I could do to attend his school instead. But it didn't matter. Nothing changed. I stayed right where I was, forced to face the daily taunts and teasing alone. I didn't have friends—only laughter at my expense. And all it did was confirm what I already believed deep down: that I wasn't enough. Many things—some worse than words—happened during that time. But there are certain things I would rather keep to myself.

By the time you're still just a child, a story about who you are, has already begun forming in your mind.

For me, it started with moments that didn't seem big to anyone else—being laughed at, overlooked, dismissed, misunderstood. I didn't know how to explain it then, but those small moments carried a powerful message: You don't belong. You're not enough. You're too much. You're not safe. And that's how the dominoes started to fall. One quiet belief leads to another.

One moment of shame stacks on top of a wound already forming. One reaction from someone you trust confirms the lie you didn't even know you were telling yourself.
And the pattern begins.

The truth is these beliefs rarely show up all at once.
They creep in. Subtle. Sneaky. They are so familiar that you don't even question them.

You live your life as if they're true.
And unless something interrupts the cycle—someone sees you, helps you unlearn, or you find your way back to your truth—it keeps going. It builds. It spirals. It becomes the lens through which you see the world and yourself.

It's not always dramatic.

Sometimes, it's just quiet damage.

Invisible fractures. Beliefs are so old you don't even notice them anymore.

But they're there. And if you don't go back to heal them, they follow you into every relationship, every opportunity, every mirror you look in. That's what this chapter has taught me: Our earliest wounds may not scream. But they never stop whispering. Until we finally decide to get help.

Reflection: Meeting the Pain

What were some ways you coped with pain when you were younger? Are you still using any of those methods today? When I was little, I lived in a storm of anxiety, panic attacks, and horrible nightmares. I was also a very angry little girl. I began calling myself cruel names, ridiculing myself—just to beat others to it. If I hurt myself first, maybe it wouldn't sting so bad when others did. When I was a teenager, I started cutting myself. That became my security blanket. If things got too bad, I told myself I had the power to end it right there. That gave me a sense of control I couldn't find anywhere else.

I also became an alcoholic before I even graduated high school. I hated the taste, but I loved the numbness. The quiet. The nothingness. Feeling nothing was the closest thing to peace I could find.

Even today, I still deal with panic attacks and a deep-rooted fear that people don't like me. That part of me hasn't fully let go. But now I know how to look at things differently.

Now, I recognize when my past is leaking into my present—and I know what to do. Prayer, meditation, visualization, and EFT have become my lifelines.

What emotion do you struggle most to allow yourself to feel? Why do you think that is?

The hardest emotion for me is self-love—specifically, loving myself without needing others to love me first. That still hurts. After a lifetime of abandonment and rejection, I've learned to assume people won't like me before they've even met me. I walk into rooms with an attitude of, "Well, they'll probably hate me too." It's not fair to me— but it became a defense mechanism. When I dig into that belief, I feel a lot of anger, but I know that behind the anger is a steady river of tears. I'm getting closer to letting them flow. Because learning to love myself, truly love myself, might be one of the most important things I ever do.

When you think about your younger self in pain, what does she need most from you today?

She needs comfort. Reassurance. Someone to tell her, "It's going to be okay." She needs to be heard and seen. She needs hugs.
She needs love—gentle, unconditional, unwavering love.

What would it look like to become a safe place for your inner child?

When I think about being that safe place for my Inner girls, the first words that come to mind are hope, security, and peace. And when I visualize that, something happens inside me, I feel powerful. I feel grounded. I feel safe, too.

Because creating a safe space for them also creates one for me.

Bonus Journal Prompts. *(Understanding emotional pain, unhealthy coping, and your inner child's needs)*

1.   **What's one unhealthy coping method you've used that you now recognize was rooted in pain—not weakness?**

Think about how you used to numb or avoid emotional pain. Can you see now how that method was a survival mechanism, not a character flaw?

How can you hold that part of yourself with more compassion?

2.   **What is one small way you can show love to your inner child today?** Maybe it's a moment of quiet, a bath, a journal session, or even saying out loud, "You didn't deserve what happened."

What does she need most right now—and how can you show up for her in a loving way?

Chapter 3 – The Weight I Wasn't Meant to Carry

When I turned ten years old, my mom remarried. I wasn't used to having a father figure—my entire life had been spent living at my grandmothers with my aunt and uncle. In my ten-year-old eyes, my mother had brought me into a marriage with a man I didn't know and taken me away from the only home I had ever known. I felt lost. She had someone—and I had no one.

When my mom packed up our things to leave my grandmother's house and move in with my new stepfather, I remember feeling a deep wave of insecurity wash over me. It was the kind of fear that didn't have words back then—but I can describe it now. Imagine placing a six-year-old, full of energy and absolutely no driving experience, behind the wheel of a car at a busy intersection. At the same time, you sit helplessly in the passenger seat. That tight-chested, wide-eyed feeling of "Oh no, this can't end well." My world, the only one I knew, was being uprooted, and I was being placed in an unknown situation. It didn't feel like a fresh start.

And looking back now, I can see that the same feeling I had in that moment—the panic of being unsteady, uncertain, and out of control—was the very energy I carried with me as I grew up. I was insecure in myself. In my abilities. In my worth. That insecurity, though invisible to me, was often visible to others. And some people—especially the strong, grounded ones—could sense it. Maybe that's why I was treated as if I was fragile or easily dismissed. It wasn't just how I saw the world but also how it was seeing me.

At age thirteen, my mother had a baby—my brother Jon. I loved caring for him. Babies brought me joy, and I welcomed the role. But things began to change. Two years later, my sister Amanda was born when I was fifteen, followed by my sister Penny when I was seventeen. Suddenly, I wasn't just the oldest child—I was a second mother. While I was in high school, already feeling like a loser and completely undeserving of friendships or confidence, I was also caring for three small children.

I stayed in my bedroom as many teenagers do, but whenever I came to the living room, I often found my mom, stepdad, and their three children settled close on the couch. All together—like one little family. And though no one said it out loud, the message was clear to me: I was on the outside looking in. I told myself my mom had a new family, and I was not a part of it. I never hated my siblings. I loved them and still do.

At that point, the emotional weight I carried found a new outlet. The pain I had buried inside began to surface in a different, darker way. When the pressure became too much, I coped by carrying a blade in my purse—my secret, silent relief. I would cut in places hidden beneath my clothes: my arms, legs, stomach, and back. That blade became my security blanket. When the world felt too heavy, when I couldn't hold it all anymore, I had something I could control. And in that twisted sense of control, I thought I had found relief.

Toward the end of my high school years, I began dating—and that's when I met my High School Sweetheart. We dated for a few years, and although life eventually took us in different directions, our story didn't end there. After breaking up and spending many years apart, we found our way back to each other in 2009. Today, my High School Sweetheart is my husband.

We've talked about my past many times. What always surprises me is how much of it he remembers—and how much I don't. I'll look through old high school yearbooks and not even recognize moments I was part of. He's told me I often had to bring my siblings along on our dates.

Before I graduated high school, I was already drinking. Vodka, cheap wine—whatever I could get my hands on. Stan, being older, could buy it for me. It wasn't about partying. It was about escaping. I wasn't running toward adulthood. I was trying to numb the parts of childhood that never got to be safe.

Reflection: – Rewriting the Narrative
In what ways have you been repeating patterns that no longer serve you?

I've spent most of my life chasing love and acceptance from others. If they didn't love me back, I took it as rejection—proof that I wasn't worthy of love, friendship, or even presence. I believed if someone pulled away, it was because I was lacking, broken, and not enough. This pattern kept me stuck in cycles of abandonment, where I expected to be left before I even got close.

Have there been relationships in your life that mirrored how you were treated as a child?

Yes. Repeatedly. Broken promises. Being pushed aside. It made me feel like an afterthought, like nothing I did was good enough, just like when I was little. The pattern repeated itself in friendships, in love, and even in professional environments. Every time it happened; it felt like the same old wound was being reopened—and I bled in silence.

What does your self-talk sound like on a hard day? Would you speak to a child that way?

My self-talk has been brutal. I've said things to myself that I wouldn't say to anyone else—especially not a child.

"I hate you." "You're worthless." "You're meant to be alone." And in those dark moments, I believed it. I meant every word.

When that pain got too loud, the thoughts of suicide would return.

Not dramatically—but quietly.

A whisper in the back of my mind: Maybe I just wasn't meant to be here. And if you've read my earlier reflections… you know that I didn't just think it. I acted on it. I carried it. I survived it.

If you could change one belief you've carried about yourself since childhood, what would it be?

I am not worthless.

I am capable—not just of surviving but of thriving.

I don't need people to define my worth or validate my existence. I can create joy, safety, and love in my life—with or without their approval. That I deserve to be here.

What qualities do you have now that your inner child would be proud of?

I want better. Not perfect—but better. I want to be in control of my emotions—not ruled by them.

Bonus Journal Prompts (Uncovering patterns, painful beliefs, and the roots of your self-talk)

1.   What pattern in your life feels hardest to break? Where do you think it started?

Is it people-pleasing? Self-criticism? Fear of rejection?

Try to trace the emotion—not to blame anyone, but to understand what you were trying to survive.

2.   If you were to rewrite your inner voice, what would you want it to say more often?

Imagine your self-talk as a best friend or nurturing parent. What messages would genuinely support you, even on the hard days?

Chapter 4 – The Ache for Connection

"Now that I've shared some of the emotional roots of my story, I want to take you deeper into what that looked like in real life. These next chapters share the healing and the experiences that shaped the girl I was—and the woman I've become."

The ache to belong somewhere was deep. At that age, most children don't understand emotional wounds or how they shape our behavior. I certainly didn't. When I heard someone say they had "emotional problems," I thought it meant they cried too much or were on the verge of being sent to a mental hospital. I feared Somone finding out that I was hurting myself.

That fear may have haunted me, but the idea of losing the one thing that helped me cope scared me more. As strange as it sounds, cutting gave me a twisted sense of comfort. Nobody cared about me—or so I believed. Nobody wanted me. So why would they want to remove the one thing that relieved me?

I had so much pain layered under that thinking. Fear. Anger. Loneliness. And the worst part was, I didn't even realize I was surviving. I thought I was living.

After I finally graduated high school, I went to college. I received a full music scholarship. The irony was that while I could sing, I was terrified to do it in front of anyone. I took private voice lessons with no confidence whatsoever. I sang in the choir all four years, entered talent shows, and sang in church—each time, the terror came with me. One would think I was a glutton for punishment.

Looking back now, I can say it honestly: I could sing. There was nothing wrong with my voice. But the laughter I grew up with—the kind that was never explained, never softened—followed me into my adult life. It wasn't just background noise. It became the story I told myself: there's something wrong with you.

Our high school choir gave students the opportunity to perform solos, duets, trios, and quartets. We rehearsed, learned our music, and, on the day of the competition, performed in front of college professors to be graded. Throughout my four years, I received red ribbons for excellence and blue ribbons for superior performance. Some students didn't place at all.

But I never connected the dots. I never gave myself credit. I chalked up my success to luck. My self-perception was so damaged that I couldn't even see what was right in front of me.
Looking back on where I am now, I wish I could go back and tell that younger version of me to believe in herself. If I had just trusted my ability, my path might have looked very different. Instead, I'm here—older, wiser, and finally realizing how deeply I was wounded. Writing

this book isn't just telling my story. It's uncovering how much of my life was shaped by those old beliefs—and how they held me back.

I would also tell my younger self to set goals to create a good life and stop focusing so much on making friends. I regret that part of my life. If I could go back in time, school would be very different. I recently pulled out my old high school yearbook to see if I could reconnect with the girl I used to be.

And there I was—my photo in black and white, barely smiling, tucked between names I barely recognized. But instead of memories flooding back, there was nothing. I couldn't remember being there. It was not the classes, teachers, conversations, laughter, awkward dances, or lunch tables. It was just a hollow blank space, as if I'd read about high school in a book but never lived it.

I stared at my face—my own eyes—and felt like I was looking at a stranger.
"Was I there?"
That was when I realized how deeply I had dissociated from my life. I had been there in body but not in spirit. The younger me had learned how to disappear from herself to stay safe. She smiled for pictures, followed routines, and walked through hallways—but she wasn't present. Not because she didn't care.

But because being present in a world that never truly cared about her was just too painful.

Even now, as I work through healing and remember pieces of my story, there are years I can't fully touch. It's like they live behind a locked door inside my mind. And I've learned that it's okay. I don't need to remember every detail to honor the girl who lived through it all.

Because what matters more than memory… is compassion.
And I choose to give that to her now, even if I can't give her back the moments she lost.

Anything I needed to do for myself, I had to figure out on my own. I had to push past to grow. I fought hard to become independent. But when adulthood finally came, I stepped into it completely unprepared. It felt like walking into a pitch-black room—no map, no flashlight and a striking fear. I was afraid of my own shadow. Every decision felt dangerous, like there were landmines scattered around me, and one wrong move would blow everything apart.

There was no guide. No reassurance.
It was me stumbling through the dark, hoping I'd somehow survive.

The small town I grew up in had shielded me from the real world, so I fell for everything when I left. My personality was dull, but I remember having a heart of gold. I loved easily. I wanted so badly to be loved back. I wanted to belong somewhere. I wanted to be wanted.

But the more I chased those things, the more distressed I became. I didn't understand what I was doing. I was acting from desire, not from truth. Others probably saw it and thought I was unstable. Looking back, I can see how off my logic was—but then, it was survival. I was doing the best I could with what I had.

I didn't return home for a long time. The memories—the stress, the tension—were too heavy to carry. As I said before, school was never easy for me—and that struggle continued into my college years. Learning didn't come naturally. Reading was still tricky, and my confidence in academic settings was low. But even with all that, I still had dreams.

A couple of years after college, I decided I wanted to work in the travel industry. Something about it felt exciting—the possibility of freedom, exploration, and helping others experience the world.

I enrolled in a Travel School that offered hands-on training in all areas of the industry—airlines, hotels, cruises, and tour companies. You name it, they covered it. They promised that if you had a dream of working in travel, they'd help you get there.

For the first time in a long time, I was on a path that made sense. It wasn't traditional. It didn't follow the typical route. But it sparked something inside of me—and that was enough to keep going.

During my time in Travel School, I met a lady who would become a long-standing friend. We hit it off quickly, laughing, dreaming, stepping into adulthood with wide eyes and open hearts. Life brought us together when we both needed a connection, and in many ways, we grew into ourselves side by side.

Over the years, we shared countless memories—some lighthearted, some complicated. We went on double dates, took spontaneous road trips (including one all the way to Wyoming with a couple of guys), and filled our days with the kind of adventures only two young, single women could create. We lived out our single years with laughter, curiosity, and a touch of rebellion.

But of all those memories, one stands out above the rest.
When I went into labor with my son, she was the one who took me to the hospital. She didn't hesitate. She stayed by my side the entire time, through every contraction, every moment of fear and anticipation, until he arrived. She was right there—offering comfort, strength, and stability when I needed it most.
We are still friends, and I will never forget the joy she brought into my life. Sometimes, the people who walk with us through life bring

both challenge and comfort, but when their presence becomes a part of your story in such a meaningful way, you hold onto that. And I always will.

Sometimes, the people in our lives don't always show up the way we wish they would in every season. But when it mattered most, she was there. And for that, I will always be grateful.

I started dating more seriously around the age of 28. I will not give names, but he still lived with his mother. He drank and used drugs. He couldn't keep a steady job but could sing and play guitar beautifully. And for me, that felt like home.

It wasn't a healthy home—but it was a home that made sense based on how I saw myself. I thought I had finally found a family. I believed I belonged there.

The truth was, I never looked at people who had it together. Somewhere deep down, I didn't think I deserved that kind of life. I assumed I belonged where the pain was—because it was all I had ever known.

The early to late '90s were a blur of searching—searching for love, belonging, and stability that I had never known. I was constantly trying to fit in and find my place in a world that never seemed to have a seat for me at the table.

I was supposed to be building a life—finding direction, planning a future. But the truth is, my mind wasn't in sync with that idea. I was still broken, still trying to survive, and I made choices from that brokenness.

At 29, I got married. Our relationship was chaotic—on again, off again—for three years. We constantly broke up and got back together, convincing ourselves we could make it work. We thought we were doing what people do: try, fall, get back up, repeat.
I got pregnant at 31. And although I did my share of drinking and smoking cigarettes, I gave them up when I found out I was going to be a mom.

Three months into the pregnancy, I had to go out of town for work. I was a marketing director for a chiropractic clinic, and we had a weekend assignment. Before I left, I asked my husband to please take care of a few things—check on our broken car and pick up my paycheck. I trusted him with that.

Instead, he took another woman to the casinos.
The couple went In my car.
They used my whole paycheck.
They spent the entire thing.

I found out through a friend. Of course, he denied it at first, but eventually, the truth came out.

And I told him goodbye. This time—for good.

I was pregnant. I was scared. And I knew deep in my soul that I couldn't let my baby grow up in that kind of chaos. That was my line in the sand.

The very next day, I tried to go to work. My car stalled in the middle of a busy intersection, and I missed work entirely. The tow truck was expensive, and I had no money—he had spent every dollar at the casinos and never once got the car fixed.

I was stuck.

No transportation.

No support.

No answers.

And truthfully? I blamed myself.

I carried the shame. I told myself this was all my fault—every bit of it. And I still believe that to this day. I could have made better choices.

What should've been a sacred time—carrying a child—was instead filled with judgment, screaming, abandonment, and rejection from people who were supposed to love me. I walked through that pregnancy with a wrecked heart and a shattered sense of self-worth. I felt hated. I felt utterly alone.

And the truth is I was.

Throughout my pregnancy, my husband had promised to keep health insurance active for both me and the baby. But that promise—like so many others—was broken.

Shortly after my son was born, I was recovering in my hospital room from a C-section when I got a call from the front desk. The voice on the other end was kind, but the news hit me like a punch to the stomach:
"Your insurance expired a few months ago." I was stunned. I had no idea.

He had quit his job without telling me—and never bothered to speak. Now, instead of resting and bonding with my newborn, I was left staring at a mountain of medical bills I had no way of paying. I had a healing body, a vulnerable baby, and a heart full of fear. Once again, I was trapped—abandoned when I needed support the most.

My doctor had told me clearly that I needed at least six weeks to heal after my C-section. The first two weeks, especially, were critical. I had stitches, a fragile body, and a newborn who needed me just as much as I needed rest.

But I couldn't afford to wait that long.

After just three weeks, I pushed myself to return to work—exhausted, hurting, and still hurting emotionally and physically. I returned to the only place I knew, hoping they would understand. But they had already made up their minds.

My position required long, demanding hours—9 a.m. to 9 p.m., five to six days a week. I worked hard—I always had—but as a brand-new single mother, my employer knew I wouldn't be able to keep up that pace. I was let go.

Suddenly, I was a new mom, still healing, with no income and no support. The father of my child had disappeared from responsibility, never paid a dime of child support, and left me to carry everything on my own.

Now, I had to find a new job fast, and it had to be enough to cover rent, bills, food, diapers, and everything my child and I needed to survive. There was no time to process, no time to grieve—just pressure to keep going when I had nothing left in me.

I remember sinking into a deep depression. Everything around me felt dull and meaningless. I lost interest in the things I used to care about, and even simple thoughts felt hard to hold onto. My mind was foggy, heavy, and full of self-doubt.

I felt like a failure—like I had let everyone down. What few relationships I still had seemed to be slipping away, and I began to believe the worst about myself: "You're a burden. You're not enough. You're messing everything up."

There was a tiny life depending on me now. And no matter how lost I felt, I knew I had to keep going—if not for me, then for him. Over the last several years, my mom and I gotten very close. One day, she asked if I'd like to move into my grandma's old home. It had been sitting empty, and she thought I could bring a little life back into it. So, my son and I moved in.

My Mom stepped in, along with my two sisters and helped by watching him while I worked in the city, and for a while, things were okay. But inside, my self-esteem was still deeply beaten down. I often felt like I was running on autopilot—doing what needed to be done but feeling disconnected from everything around me.

Still, I kept moving. I didn't have the energy to dream or the confidence to thrive, but I had a little boy who needed me—and that was enough to keep going.

I did my best to do the right things through all of it. I showed up. I worked hard. And even though I felt like I was failing in so many areas, I knew one thing for sure: I was a devoted mom. And if I failed at everything else, I was grateful that this wasn't one of them.

Reflection: – Facing the Truth
What parts of yourself did you feel you had to hide to be accepted?

Everything.

My smile—because I didn't like it.

My body—because I never felt pretty.

My personality—because I was too afraid of saying the wrong thing. I wasn't used to being around people, so I held back from speaking up. If I stay quiet, maybe I won't be judged. If I don't speak, I can't say anything wrong—right? So I stayed in the corner.

That's where I thought it was safest. But the truth is I was hiding from life. And from myself.

When did you first learn to stop asking for help? How did that shape your life?

I'm still learning this one.

I have someone who's helping me and counseling me, and it's making a powerful difference. This healing teaches me to become firm, so asking for help becomes a choice… not a cry from desperation.

What does "abandonment" mean to you—not just from others, but from yourself?

Abandonment feels like being tossed away—like trash.

It's brutal. It's a pain without a name.

It's the feeling of being left behind and never looked back on.

And when I've abandoned myself, it's been just as painful.

When I ignored what I needed, silenced my voice, or begged for love from people who couldn't give it, I left myself behind.

How have you abandoned your own needs to keep the peace or be liked?

This question stings because it's been a massive part of my life.

I spent years trying to be liked, fit in, and be accepted.

And in the process, I lost so much time.

I could have used the time to grow, heal, and build something beautiful.

Instead, I chased love like it was a finish line.

And now, looking back, I see all the things I missed while doing it.

But I forgive myself because I know better now.

What's one way you can begin showing up for yourself differently this week?

I can give myself space. Silence.

I can sit with just me—and not run from the quiet.

I love visualization. I love meditation. And when unwanted emotions surface, I'm ready to show them the door.

I'm also committing to journaling and devotional work with God this week. Because spending time with Him is how I remember who I am. And who I'm becoming.

Bonus Journal Prompts (Facing abandonment, survival roles, and self-sacrifice)

1.   When have you abandoned yourself to keep someone else comfortable?

What did it cost you?

What would it have felt like to choose yourself in that moment instead?

2.   What does showing up for yourself look like today in small and realistic ways? (*Think simple. A walk. A boundary. A deep breath. A moment of prayer.*)

Write a list of 3–5 ways you can care for yourself like someone you genuinely love.

Chapter 5 – When the Mask Starts to Slip

After a couple of years of living in my hometown, I knew something had to change. I needed to create a better life for me and my son—more financial stability and time together. I took a bold step and reached out to a company in another state. There wasn't even a job posted, but my background in sales and marketing impressed them enough to create a position they didn't know they needed. It was a leap of faith, and I took it.

This move was huge—for both of us. My son was six at the time, and together, we packed up and moved four hours away. I was earning more than I ever had, and everything was close: his school, my job, our home—all within ten minutes of each other. For the first time, life felt manageable, peaceful, and empowering. We lived there from 2007 to 2009; during that time, I felt stronger and more confident than ever.

Then, one night, everything shifted again.
I found out that my old high school sweetheart was divorced. Something about hearing that stirred something deep inside me: I hadn't spoken to him in years, but I felt compelled to reach out. So, I called.

We talked, and it felt natural—like no time had passed. Our conversation had a familiarity, a comfort I hadn't felt in a long time.

We started spending time together again, and the connection we once had grew. I had always regretted how things ended between us. Back then, I had let other people's voices speak louder than my own. They told me he wasn't right for me, and I listened because I didn't know how to trust myself. I was so used to being told what to do, how to feel, and when to breathe that I didn't realize I was allowed to think for myself. But this time was different.

I was older. Wiser. And slowly learning how to trust my own heart.

In 2009, we got married. I was never one for long engagements, and this time, we didn't feel the need to second-guess what we already believed deep down: God intended for us to be together.

He was still living in our hometown, and with three children from his previous marriage, he didn't want to move far from them. As a mother, I respected that. So, I moved back home to the place I had once fought so hard to leave behind.

What I didn't realize then was that with that move, the torment was about to begin all over again.

Still, part of me believed this was my second chance. We hadn't dated while he was married—this wasn't a story of infidelity but one of reconnection. It felt like God had reopened a door, and I walked through it with hope in my heart, thinking, This time, we'll get it right.

But I wasn't just stepping into a marriage—I was stepping into a complex reality. My husband's ex-wife deeply resented me. And his children, and my child, all close in age—5, 9, 9½, and 12—came with their own needs, hurts, and dynamics. On top of that, he had recently been diagnosed with dilated cardiomyopathy, a serious heart condition that left him unable to work. He was preparing to go on disability.

Suddenly, I wasn't just starting a new life.
I was taking on a role filled with unexpected weight and responsibility.

In truth, I didn't fully understand what I was walking into. That was my fault. I tended to jump headfirst into things, driven more by heart than caution. My husband is a wonderful man—a good Christian man—and I love him. But I was still too weak inside and broken to handle everything that came with this new chapter. In many ways, I failed in that part of the journey.

I had to find a job again, which wasn't easy at the time—and I was back to commuting, something I had grown used to not doing. My husband's kids came over every other weekend, and I genuinely wanted them to feel at home with their father. Even with my limited income, I did everything I could to ensure they had what they needed—individual beds, fresh bedding, toys, clothes, and anything else to help them feel comfortable, safe, and welcomed.

I opened my heart to those kids. I had fun with them. I wanted them to know they were loved. But there were challenges I hadn't anticipated. Each visit often began with them repeating harsh things their mother had said about us.

At that time, I was still emotionally immature. I hadn't yet developed the tools to manage that kind of tension and emotional warfare. So, I did what I now regret—I started saying things back. Not because I wanted to hurt anyone but because I didn't know how to respond from a place of strength. I look back now and wish I had done better—not for her sake, but for the kids. They didn't deserve to be caught in the middle of grown-up pain and dysfunction. And in my way, I contributed to that chaos. That's something I will always carry—and something I have worked hard to grow from.

We decided to become members of a local church. I hadn't grown up attending regularly, so this was a new chapter for me. I had always believed in Christ, but consistency in church involvement hadn't been part of my earlier life.
At first, it felt right—a fresh start, a place to grow. But looking back, I wish we hadn't taken on leadership roles so quickly. That's where the problems began.

The church asked my husband and me to serve as youth directors. He led Sunday school lessons every Sunday morning and again on Wednesday and Sunday nights. I stood beside him during those sessions, helping however I could. We also took the kids to youth camp every year—a wonderful experience that I still hold dear. Then, during a women's conference, the topic of Vacation Bible School came up. The leader asked if anyone would be willing to serve as the VBS director. No one raised their hand. After a moment of hesitation, I nervously slipped mine up and said, "I'll do it." How hard could it be? I can handle this… right?

Shortly after, I met with the preacher's wife, who had run VBS the year before. She gave me the lay of the land—and a warning. "Whatever you do," she said, "don't micromanage. Once people have their departments, let them run their show." I nodded. "No problem."

Then she added something that stuck with me: "The Last time I directed, they were so mean I left in tears. They destroyed me." That should have been a red flag, but I brushed it off. This is the church, I thought. How bad can it get?
I divided up the departments and let everyone have their space. I was left with the children's entertainment area, which was fine with me. The theme was Carnival, so I set up booths in the gym, each with little games and stations. To manage the flow, I tried to stagger the

lunch breaks so that kids would rotate and I could keep things organized, but I was overruled by a lady that wasn't there initially to be the director.

One afternoon, while I was working on the Carnival set up in the gym, three women stood nearby, silently watching me. I didn't think much of it until the next day when I returned, I found that my entire setup had been knocked down. I was angry and hurt, but I kept going. I rebuilt everything and had it ready in time for the first day of VBS.

That first day went smoothly. I stayed in the cafeteria until the last child got on the bus, and then I left for work. But the next day, everything unraveled.

While making my rounds and blowing up balloons for the kids, one of the women called me over. I thought she needed help—but instead, she gave me a piece of her mind. Her tone was sharp, and her words cut deep. Her last thing still echoes in my memory: "If you were any kind of director, you would know that."
I was stunned. Speechless. I turned around and walked away. I went straight to the woman who had unofficially tried to take over as director and told her, "I quit."

She looked at me and said, "You quit? You can't quit! Where were you yesterday?"

I stared at her, confused. "I was here," I said. "All day. I stayed until the last bus left."

She snapped back, "No, you were not!"
So, I walked her into the cafeteria and asked one of the workers, "Was I here yesterday when the last group of kids left?"
The worker nodded. "Yes. She stayed until the last bus pulled out."
After that, the woman had nothing to say—except to inform me that she had gathered my group of volunteers for a meeting afterward, and I hadn't shown up. I told her I never knew about any meeting. No one told me. Not to mention—why was she calling meetings when she wasn't the director?

That experience shook something in me.
I didn't go back after that, and to this day, I've struggled to return to any church regularly. It's not that I lost my faith—I didn't. I still believe in Christ, I still pray, and I still feel His presence.
But the pain I felt from people inside those walls left a scar. Church was supposed to be a sanctuary—a place of love, growth, and acceptance. Instead, I was humiliated, dismissed, and made to feel small by people who claimed to follow Jesus.

That experience didn't turn me away from God. It just made me hesitant to trust people who say they represent Him.

Reflection: – From Surviving to Thriving
What does thriving look like for you now—and how is it

different from surviving?

Thriving feels satisfying and scary—all at once.

It means you're doing something worthwhile, something meaningful,

something with purpose.

But it also means stepping into the unknown.

That's what makes it different from surviving. Surviving is

predictable, familiar—even if it's painful.

Thriving is unpredictable. But I now believe I have the power to do

it.

In what ways have you settled for less because you believed you

weren't worthy of more?

I have settled for less almost every single day of my life.

Not because I didn't try to reach for more—but because when I did,

I never felt like I belonged there.

I'm learning that I am worthy of more, even if I don't always feel like

it.

Write a letter from your future self—what does she want you to stop carrying?

Dear Me,

Please stop counting on people to carry you.

Stop chasing love that won't stay. Live your life.

You were made for great things—deep down, you know that. But you'll never experience the full depth of your purpose if you're more concerned with being liked than being whole.

Choose yourself. I promise the love you're looking for will follow.

Think about someone who made you feel "less than." What would you say to them now, with strength and grace?

With strength, I can say this:

You made me feel less than I truly am.

You thought you knew me, but you didn't.

I am a child of God—made in His image, wonderfully created.

And He loves me just as much as He loves you.

I'm sorry you felt the need to dim my light.

But I'm no longer shrinking to make you comfortable.

I'm moving on now—with grace and truth in my hands.

What small truth are you ready to live out loud? I
am allowed to be kind to myself.

I can practice self-compassion—especially when I want to tear myself
down.

I can set boundaries to protect my well-being, and I don't need
anyone's permission to do so.

That truth? I'm ready to live it. Out loud. In peace. And without

apology.

Bonus Journal Prompts

(From surviving to thriving, self-worth, and seeing your future differently)

1.   What does "thriving" mean to you—personally, not by anyone else's definition?

Forget what the world says. What does your thriving look like in daily life, in your spirit, in your relationships?

2.   How do you talk to yourself in moments of success versus moments of struggle?

Do you celebrate yourself when you win? Do you comfort yourself when you fall? What would it look like to treat both moments with grace?

Chapter 6 – Whispers From Within

It didn't happen all at once. There wasn't some dramatic awakening or lightning bolt moment. The shift was quiet. I almost missed it.

At first, it came as restlessness. A hollow ache would appear in the quiet hours when no one needed me and the noise had died. I'd feel it in my chest or my gut—this stirring I didn't understand. It wasn't anxiety exactly, and it wasn't sadness either. It was something in between, something more profound.

Looking back now, I know what it was: it was her. My inner child. The younger version of me I had spent decades trying to ignore, hide, or outgrow. She had been there all along, carrying everything I couldn't deal with at the time—fear, shame, rejection, loneliness. And now, she wanted to be seen.

I didn't know how to listen to her at first. I didn't even realize it was her. I just felt overwhelmed, like emotions were trying to pour out of me but didn't have a name or direction. Sometimes, I'd cry without knowing why. Other times, I'd feel anger bubble up over the most minor things. But underneath it all was that whisper. Something in me wanted to be held, not judged and comforted, not fixed.

It was around that time I started Googling things—phrases like "Emotional pain," "depression," and "why do I feel empty."

"According to several mental health sources like the Mayo Clinic and NIMH, the symptoms of depression and anxiety can be broken down into emotional, cognitive, physical, and behavioral categories." When I read through them for the first time, they hit me like a ton of bricks. Symptom after symptom, list after list, it was like someone had written my life out on a screen.

Emotional Symptoms:

- Persistent sadness, low mood, or emptiness

- Feelings of hopelessness, worthlessness, or guilt

- Loss of interest or pleasure in activities once enjoyed

- Irritability, anxiety, or agitation

- Cognitive Symptoms:

- Difficulty concentrating, remembering, or making decisions

- Slowed thinking or speech

- Confusion or forgetfulness

- Thoughts of death or suicide

Physical Symptoms:

• Changes in appetite (loss or gain)

• Sleep disturbances (insomnia, oversleeping)

• Fatigue or lack of energy

• Physical aches and pains (e.g., headaches, back pain)

Behavioral Symptoms:

• Withdrawal from social activities

• Neglecting personal hygiene or appearance

• Difficulty functioning in work, school, or relationships

• Increased substance use (e.g., alcohol, drugs)

I could've written that list myself. It was as if someone had entered my mind and put it all into words, I didn't know I needed.

That's also when I started to realize something else—something big. Emotional abuse? It can be just as damaging—if not worse—than physical abuse. And I would have never known. Where I came from, emotional pain was something you "sucked up." There was no time to feel sorry for yourself. If you mentioned struggling, someone would quickly remind you of others who had it worse: the homeless, the abused, the forgotten. The message was always clear—don't complain.

While thinking of others is a beautiful and admirable quality, I finally came to the realization that you can't honestly care for others if you're hurting. There comes a time in your life when you must stop and tend to yourself—not out of selfishness but out of necessity. Healing isn't self-centered—it's foundational. When you begin caring for yourself with compassion and intention, you gain the strength and clarity to love others more fully and contribute meaningfully to the world around you.

And that's when I knew—I couldn't keep going like this. Something had to change. Even though I didn't know how to fix what was broken, I was finally willing to try.

That willingness to face the pain, grow, and heal led me to explore Holistic Healing.

From our first session, I felt seen in a way I never had before. I began learning to listen to the parts of myself I had long silenced— the younger, wounded places buried under years of survival.

I started recognizing the emotional injuries I had carried for so long

I sat with them. I tended to them. I worked with them—every single day.

Out of respect for the sacredness of our work, I won't go into deep detail. I wouldn't be where I am today without God guiding her steps.

Her compassion was quiet but powerful.

Her insight was deep but gentle.

And her presence during that season of my life is something I will carry with gratitude forever.

Reflection: – Glimpses of God

When did you feel God's presence in the middle of your pain?

I have often felt God, but one moment still stays with me. A dear friend of mine was waiting on devastating test results, and my heart was breaking. I loved and cared for them deeply, and I was terrified.

I came home from work, went to the center of my bed, and prayed like I had never prayed before. I remember the feeling—like a net of soft light was wrapped around me, cocooning me in peace.

Every time I entered that space, I felt held. Safe.

And I knew—deep in my spirit—God was there.

That moment left a mark on me, and so did the result. The test that should have been bad came back good.

Thank You, God.

What does grace mean to you today—and how is it different from what you once believed?

Grace carries so many meanings, but for me now, it starts with self-compassion. It's treating myself with kindness, forgiveness, and understanding. Grace is what lets me release the rage I've held.

It also reminds me: I am not the ultimate judge—God is.

And He forgives all who come to Him.

Grace is also transformation. The power turns pain into purpose and suffering into growth.

It helps us make meaning from our most challenging experiences and move forward. I'm doing that now and hope to help others do the same.

In the past, I saw grace as something abstract.

Now? I see it as everything.

What did it feel like the first time you realized healing was possible?

I cried. I cried my eyes out. The very first time I used EFT, I felt the pain I was holding leave my body. It was gone after just one round. I was shocked, relieved, encouraged and still doing it today.

That was all I needed for most surface-level issues. However, my counselor helped guide me through the more profound work when we got deeper. It was real. And that changed everything.

What would some of the lyrics be if your healing journey had a soundtrack?

"The Voice of Truth" by Casting Crowns would be one of the lead tracks. That song speaks to exactly where I've been and who I'm becoming. It reminded me that even when the world and my wounds said I was weak, God's voice was reminding me that I was chosen. Strong, loved and that I would rise.

Bonus Journal Prompts (Faith, presence, grace, and the beginning of more profound healing)

1.What's one area of your life where you're still learning to accept grace?

It could be a past mistake, an ongoing struggle, or something you're still wrestling with. What does it feel like to let grace in here?

2. How would you describe God's presence in your healing journey?

Chapter 7 – My First Glimpse of Healing

Healing didn't arrive like a miracle. It came like a soft breeze—barely noticeable, but enough to make me pause and think, "Wow… I can feel something. Peace."

I didn't expect magic when I first began working with my counselor. I just hoped for something to help me breathe again. She introduced me to the EFT—Emotional Freedom Technique, or "tapping." I had never heard of it before but was willing to try anything that might relieve me.

It worked beautifully!

There was something profoundly calming about tapping on the body while speaking painful truths out loud. It helped me name what I was feeling without shame. And something about that—acknowledging the pain instead of avoiding it—was powerful. It felt like, for the first time, I wasn't pushing things down. I was letting them rise and out.

EFT gave me a sense of control in moments when I usually felt helpless. When emotions overwhelmed me, I now had something tangible I could do—something that said, "You're not powerless anymore."

I began on some of the most recent issues. Just one round and the anger and hatred were gone. I could still remember what caused it, but its weight no longer sat on my chest. That's the key—it's not about erasing the memory. It's about releasing the feeling. Feelings are important, but not all are meant to be carried forever.

Eventually, I reached the more profound layers—the ones buried the longest—and that's where healing my inner child came in.

This was the hardest part. There was so much hurt, sadness, confusion, self-doubt, and fear. Could I do this on my own? What if I got it wrong? What if I failed?

Healing your inner child is a profoundly personal journey. No one can walk it for you, but you are never truly alone. You will know when healing begins with God beside you and the right tools. You'll feel it in your spirit. You'll feel it in the quiet.

That's what this chapter of my life became: the beginning of returning home to myself.

One of my most potent realizations was that I spent so much of my life reaching for people I saw as more substantial—grounded and whole. I didn't just want to be around them. I needed them because I didn't yet see that strength within myself. I felt unworthy unless someone else reflected it to me. And when they told me, "You need to love yourself," I didn't hear the truth—I heard rejection. I thought it meant, "Go fix yourself somewhere else."

But they were trying to help me see something I wasn't ready to believe, and until I could stand in my light, I'd keep relying on others to feel worthy of love.

Friendship is about walking beside one another—not carrying each other through every step. Once I saw that, I knew it was time to finally become someone who could stand, not just lean.

And that's when something shifted in me. I felt called to go deeper— to meet the parts of me waiting the longest.

This moment taught me something sacred—something no one else could have handed me.

I had the power all along. I had the power to reclaim what was mine, step into those broken spaces, clean the house, and stand tall for the little girl who had waited so long for someone to fight for her. I realized I could step up to the plate for myself and take the wheel with confidence.

I didn't know what the next chapter would bring, but I knew one thing: My inner child was home.

I will be there for them—not just today, but every day.

Every time they have a question, a worry, or a dream, I want them to know they can come to me. I'll listen, guide them, and hold space.

I want to teach them how to open the Bible and find the truth, pray when they feel scared, and end each night with peace. We'll have our devotionals and quiet moments of faith together because I want God to be the foundation of their lives permanently.

I'll show them what love looks like. How can we love others deeply and compassionately and love ourselves with that same devotion? Because they were beautifully made. And nothing in this world can take that away.

There are still parts of me that resist being in a safe space.

My current self-doubts at times.

What if I mess up? What if I miss something important? What if I let them down?

The idea of being the one someone else counts on still scares me.

But alongside that fear, I feel something else.

Power.

The quiet kind. The kind that rises from love, intention, and choosing to show up even when you're scared.

And that's what I'm doing. I'm choosing my inner child—me—every single day.

I didn't have a perfect parenting manual—no one does. I didn't even know what tomorrow would look like. But I knew one thing—I would show up for my child daily, even if I were learning as I went along.

Reflection: – The First Glimpse

What was the first time you felt safe to let a real emotion come to the top? I felt safe when I first started meditation. The clarity I got gave me peace. I prayed and I really felt the presence of God all around me.

How do you usually react when painful feelings show up? What might it look like to respond instead?

In the past, I would hide. I didn't want to be around people when I felt low—so I would retreat. I'd sit with the pain, grovel in it, let it grow. I gave it room to stay far too long. But now I don't do that anymore.

Now, I meet the pain differently. If it shows up, I acknowledge it. I feel it. I honor it. Then I kindly show it the door. It's not allowed to linger in my life anymore.

What have you been carrying that you're now ready to release?

There are memories—ones I've processed with my counselor—that are painful. I've acknowledged them. I've faced them. I've done the work. And now, I've decided: those memories will stay locked away in Julie's memory vault.

I'm not avoiding them. I no longer need to revisit them to prove my healing. They're no longer the loudest voices in the room.

In what ways has God shown up for you during your healing—even quietly?

I know God is always with me through faith—but there were moments when I felt Him. Especially when this journey first began.

A stillness, peace, and a holy presence told me I wasn't walking this alone. Even now, in the quiet moments, I can feel Him there.

Sometimes, He shows up in peace. Sometimes, He shows up in the people who speak life into me. And sometimes, He shows up in me.

Bonus Journal Prompts

(Your first glimpse of healing, EFT, and emotional release)

1.What was one emotion you used to fear—and what have you learned about it now?

Is there a feeling that used to overwhelm or scare you?

What have you discovered about its roots, and how are you beginning to respond to it differently?

2. What does "emotional freedom" mean to you right now?
Describe what it looks like, feels like, or sounds like. What would it change if you gave yourself full permission to feel and release instead of hold and hide?

Chapter 8– A Moment of Awakening

There's something I need to say—to myself and to the little girls I've brought home. Not all pain is about the present moment. Some of it is old and buried, replaying itself in new familiar situations, even when they're not.

The other night, I felt that old ache rise again—that hollow, hopeless feeling of being unwanted, unchosen, and invisible. I saw myself being rejected again. I thought I wasn't good enough to be loved by someone in my life. But then, something softened inside me. A whisper rose from the truth:

This pain isn't about today.

This feeling is the past knocking on the door again.

Because the truth is—that special someone didn't reject me. This person never made promises they didn't keep. They showed up exactly how they said they would, and they're still here in the way they committed to being. They never promised me things would be as perfect as I expected. And just because I hoped for something more doesn't mean they failed me—or I failed myself.

It means I felt a familiar ache, and I had the chance to respond differently this time.

So, I turned inward. I found my girls—the five-year-old, the eight-year-old—and I spoke with kindness: "I know this hurts. I know it feels familiar. But not everyone will leave you. Not everyone will forget you. Some people will show up— and stay exactly how they said they would. This isn't rejection, sweetheart. This is just an old wound trying to feel seen."

That was when I realized healing isn't just about love and softness. It's about gently correcting the old stories when they try to take over again. It's about learning to see clearly, even through tears.

And I reminded my inner girls, with all the love in my heart: "It's okay to hope. It's okay to feel. And it's okay to learn. We're still healing—and that's what makes us brave."

Being married has been rough sometimes.

My husband has always told me how to do things around the house. Whether it's folding the laundry or sweeping the floor, he always has an opinion. And while some people might brush that off, it's always landed hard for me. Not because I think he's trying to hurt me—but because deep down, it taps into something much older.

At first, I just felt angry. But behind the anger was sadness.

Growing up, I never felt like I measured up. I struggled in school and work environments. My low self-esteem made me believe I wasn't capable. I second-guessed myself constantly, and when I failed, it only proved the lie my inner child already believed: You're not good enough.

So now, in my adult life, even when someone I love gives a suggestion or a correction—it doesn't land as help. It lands as criticism. As if the little girl inside me heard, "You still don't know what you're doing. You still don't measure up."

And I react—not always with grace because that old pain is still there.

I'm learning now that my reaction isn't about him. It's about the wounded part of me that still doesn't believe she's capable, competent, or enough.

But I'm also learning this: I can respond different when I pause and see where the pain is coming from. I can take a breath. I can reassure my inner child that she's not failing. She's learning. She's safe. And she's doing beautifully.

Yes, it starts hurting.

Yes, it may not be very clear.

Yes, it might feel like you're falling apart.

But you're not falling apart. You're falling into alignment.

I used to think my world was falling apart — but it turns out God was realigning me. Things had to come undone so I could go home to who I truly am

What's surfacing isn't breaking you—it's leaving you. It's rising so you can love, hold, and then release it. And it only comes because you've built enough internal safety to handle it now.

This is the beginning of true emotional alchemy. You're not suppressing anymore. You're honoring.

Reflection: – Reclaiming My Inner Girls

When you visualize your inner child(ren), what do they look like? What are they doing?

I've taken in two little girls—two versions of me. One is five. She's got messy blonde hair, two missing teeth, dirt on her legs, and the kind of smile that lights up everything. She's wild and rowdy and wants to play outside in the dirt and the grass. She doesn't have time to talk—she's busy being a tomboy.

The other is eight. She has short, light brown hair. She's still a tomboy, but you can tell she's carrying something heavier. She's quieter, more serious, and more ready to sit down and listen.

Both are pieces of me. And they've come home.

What would it mean to truly become the safe space you never had?

It would mean peace and security. It would mean that I am finally powerful—not because I control everything, but because I've created a life where I feel safe. That is everything.

What scares you about being the one who holds your own heart?

My self-doubt. I still carry it around more than I'd like to admit. I fear making mistakes. I fear getting it wrong. I haven't fully conquered that yet, but I know it now. And awareness is the first step toward healing.

How does it feel to imagine giving your inner child her own space to thrive?
It feels exciting. It feels powerful. She can grow strong, confident, and free in this space. She can be anything she wants to be. And I'll be right here cheering her on.

What does "cleaning house" emotionally mean to you right now?
It means getting rid of anything that no longer belongs—negativity, fear, toxic patterns, and all the emotional clutter that prevents joy. It means making room. Room for peace. Room for creativity. Room for a life that feels good.

Bonus Journal Prompts (A moment of awakening, reclaiming power, and creating a safe inner space)

1.   **What does being a "safe space" for yourself look like in everyday life?**

Think about daily routines, conversations, or decisions. How can you continue creating an inner atmosphere that says, "You are safe here"?

2.   **What would your 5-year-old and 8-year-old selves thank you for today?**

Look at how far you've come. What are you giving them now that they never had before?

Chapter 9 – Becoming Worthy of Myself

There's a strange thing that happens when you start choosing yourself. At first, it feels unnatural. It's like you're breaking some kind of rule you didn't even know you were living by.

You speak truthfully, even if your voice trembles. And for a while, it doesn't feel good. It feels selfish, maybe a little Awkward.

But then, something shifts. You begin to realize that the life you were living wasn't yours. It was a stitched-together version of what everyone else needed you to be.

This chapter is about what happened when I started to unravel that. It's about learning how to live—not for validation, not for approval, not to avoid rejection—but simply because I am worthy of being alive, heard, and loved.

For so long, I thought I had to earn love. I thought I had to be pleasing, small, and agreeable. If I took up space or had needs, I would become too much for the people around me. And sometimes, I was treated that way. So I began to shrink, apologize, over function, and over give.

But slowly, as I kept showing up for my inner girls, something began to change. I didn't want to abandon them again. I didn't want to model that their worth depended on others' thoughts.

So I started showing them what it looked like to choose ourselves: to walk away from what hurts, to speak gently to the mirror, to honor our yes and trust our no.

This chapter is about stepping into that kind of worthiness that doesn't shout or prove.

Section 1 – "At first, choosing myself felt like a betrayal, but now I see it was love."

I knew I needed help. I was nervous about my emotional needs, and I wasn't comfortable letting people know I was getting help. So many people still laugh at things like that. They smirk, they judge, and they say things like, "Just suck it up."

But the healing I've experienced through this journey has been robust. It's changed me. It's made me a better person—more grounded, more present, more real.

I remember one day during a session with my counselor, she was talking about loving yourself. And I asked, "How do you love yourself?" It probably sounded silly, but I couldn't wrap my head around it. I genuinely didn't know.

She looked at me and said, "Well... you're doing it right now."

And that's when it clicked.

Just by getting help—just by showing up for myself—I was already loving myself.

It was a radical shift in perspective. For most of my life, I thought choosing myself would be selfish. I thought it meant I didn't care about others or was full of myself. I was embarrassed to mention that I was learning to love myself. I knew people would roll their eyes. But now?

If more people truly learned how to love themselves, we wouldn't have half the trouble in the world that we do. We'd be more compassionate.

At first, choosing myself felt like a betrayal. But now I know—it was the beginning of love.

Section 2 – "My inner girls didn't need me to be perfect. They needed me to stop abandoning them."

I, for one, am glad to have my Inner Children living with me now. The abandonment, rejection, shame, and even hatred they experienced during the early years of their lives devastated them beyond measure. No words are strong enough to describe the weight they carried for so long—alone, confused, and unseen.

But now they're not alone anymore. Being the adult, my Inner Kids have a safe place to face those recurring pains—not by erasing them, but by standing beside them. This time, we walk through the hurt together. And because of that, the story gets a different ending.

This time, the outcome is healing. This time, they get to feel seen.

This time, they cannot carry that horrible, heavy load alone.

And here's what I never realized for so long. The voice that hurt them the most wasn't always someone else's—it was mine. As I grew up, I didn't just think I wasn't enough—I said it to myself. Repeatedly.

"Julie, you're so stupid."

"I hate you."

"You're not worth anything."

"You're ugly."

"Why were you even born?" And the list went on.

I thought they were just words. I didn't know they were wounds. I didn't think they were shaping every part of me—my confidence, relationships, and ability to dream. I didn't realize those words weren't just rolling off my tongue… they were sticking. They were scarring.

I have lived a lifetime of hurting myself—physically, mentally, emotionally—without even recognizing it as pain. But my inner Children felt it all. And what they needed most wasn't a perfect version of me.

They needed me to stop abandoning them and stop turning on myself.

They needed me to become someone who could say,

"You are worth loving, even when you're hurting, even when you mess up."

And now that I'm here—I'm not going anywhere.

Section 3 – "I used to need people to like me. Now, I need to stay true to myself."

Oh my goodness, this one is hard. I needed people to like me. It wasn't just something I wanted—it was the most important thing in my life. The thought of someone not liking me could send me into a spiral that felt like the world was ending. It would stop everything. I couldn't move forward. I couldn't breathe.

Looking back, I realize how deeply I tied my worth to being accepted. Being liked felt like survival. If someone didn't like me, it wasn't just rejection—it was proof, in my mind, that something was wrong with me.

And I suffered. I suffered deeply—over people who didn't think twice about me. Over people I gave so much energy to, who barely gave me a second thought.

Honestly, I cared more about them than they cared about me.

And even more heartbreaking.

I cared more about them than I cared about me.

Let that sink in.

I believe that is the part that hurts the most—not that they didn't choose me, but that I abandoned myself in trying to be selected.

But now I'm learning a different way. Some people may not like me. And that's okay. The ones who should be with you—will love the real you, not the version you created just to fit in.

I don't need everyone to like me anymore. I need to stay true to myself.

Section 4 – "Self-worth isn't loud. It's quiet, steady, and sometimes hard to hold—but it's mine now."

Self-worth isn't loud. It doesn't scream from the rooftops. It doesn't walk into a room demanding attention or applause.

Self-worth is quiet. It's in how I speak to myself in the mirror.

It's in how I rest without guilt. It's in saying no without explaining.

It's in holding space for myself when emotions rise—without calling them "too much."

There are still days it slips through my fingers—days I question everything, days the old voices get loud again. But now, I know what it feels like to come home to myself. I know how to pause. Breathe. Reconnect.

Because self-worth is not something I perform. It's something I practice. It's quiet. It's steady. And yes—it's sometimes hard to hold. But it's mine now.

Reflection: – Choosing Me

In what ways have you chosen others over yourself—and how did that affect you? I put others first for so long—so far ahead of myself that I disappeared. I tried to be the person they wanted, needed, expected.

I overextended, over gave, over cared—just hoping they would see me, love me, stay. But the more I did that, the more I lost touch with who I was. I was chasing scraps of love while starving myself of the real thing.

What belief are you finally ready to let go of about needing to be liked? I'm ready to let go of the belief that being liked is my life's purpose. I wasn't put on this earth to be accepted by everyone. That is not my mission. My mission is to live with love, honesty, and faith.

To be kind.

To be genuine.

To give without losing myself in the process.

If others like me—that's beautiful.

If they don't—I'll still be okay.

If you fully trust your worth, how would your relationships look different? If I trusted my worth completely, I wouldn't cling to people who treat me like an option. I'd walk away from disrespect without needing to explain myself. I would protect my peace like it's sacred—because it is.

I would attract people who see me, value my heart, and know how to give as much as they receive.

How can you choose yourself this week—with love, not guilt?

This week, I will choose time alone without feeling selfish. I will do something kind for myself without overthinking it.

I'll remind myself that rest is holy, that joy is allowed, and that choosing me is not the same as abandoning anyone else.

I'm still learning, but I'm walking in love now. And that includes love for me.

Bonus Journal Prompts (Self-worth, choosing yourself, releasing the need for approval)

1.   What does "being enough" feel like in your body? What shifts when you believe it?

Take a moment to reflect on how your body responds when you genuinely believe you are enough. What softens? What tensions fade?

2.   Who are you becoming when you stop chasing approval and start choosing peace?

Describe her. What does she do differently? How does she show up? Let her become your vision.

Chapter 10 – Rising From Within

Healing doesn't just ask you to revisit the past—it invites you to rise from it, with God's hand in yours.

After walking through the pain, the memories, and the voices that tried to bury me, I started to see something I never expected: light. Not outside of me, not in another person, but in Christ. And because He lives in me, I realized that light was everywhere.

This chapter marks the moment I stopped waiting for someone else to rescue me and started trusting the One who already had. I began to see that everything I was searching for—strength, peace, belonging—was already within me because Jesus never left me. Even when I couldn't feel Him, He planted seeds I would later discover.

This new strength didn't come all at once. It came in flickers:

A verse at just the right moment.

A peace that didn't make sense.

A breath that no longer carried shame.

This chapter is about rising. Not because the pain disappeared—but because Jesus carried me through it. Because now, the story isn't just about what happened to me. It's about what I chose to become—with Him—after it.

Rooted in Something Unshakable

I've made the choice to give God the glory in all that happens in my life because it is through Him that all things are possible. He is my Rock, my safe place, and my steady ground.

When I first brought my inner girls home, I prayed for God to guide me through the rest of my life. I said, "Not my will, Lord, but Yours." I was tired—tired of fear, shame, and carrying everything on my own. What I needed wasn't more strength… it was surrender.

And that's what I gave Him.

My Pain Still Counts

For many years, I stayed silent about my past—not because it didn't hurt, but because I convinced myself it didn't "qualify." I had read so many stories of worse trauma that I began to discredit my own.

I told myself, "Other people have it harder. My pain isn't enough to matter." But pain doesn't come with a measuring stick. One day, I heard a woman share how being teased as a child had shaped her life. And for a moment, I judged her pain. That's it? I thought.

But immediately, something clicked. I was doing to this woman what I had done to myself—ranking pain, comparing wounds, trying to measure what hurts "enough" to count.

And I realized how dangerous that is.

Everyone's trauma is valid. If it silences you, shapes you, or shames you it matters. Whether the world calls it "big" or "small"—if it hurts you, it's worth healing.

I no longer need to downplay what I've carried. I don't need to tell it all. But I do need to say to myself: It mattered. And so do I.

The Shift

The moment I knew I was genuinely changing didn't come wrapped in peace—it came in a breakdown.

I had fallen into a deep wave of despair. I believed I had lost someone dear to me, and it hit me like a weight I couldn't carry. My body felt heavy. My spirit collapsed. I just wanted to lie down and disappear. But then, out of nowhere, realized that the feeling trying to take over, was an old wound trying to haunt me. It was as plain as day. I was also able to determine that the feeling I was having was not reality.

The depression suddenly lifted. I was able to move back away far enough to see this in a different perspective. I saw it for what it was.

What would've kept me down for days only stayed for a couple of hours. That was the moment I knew I had changed—not because I stopped hurting, but because I finally knew how to see my pain and respond with clarity instead of collapse.

A New Kind of Understanding

Not long after, I had another realization.

For years, whenever I asked my husband for help, he would say things like, "I don't know," or "You might want to ask someone else." And it always felt like rejection—like I wasn't significant enough to be helped directly.

But as I grew through this journey, I started to look deeper.

What if that wasn't dismissal but direction? What if he wasn't ignoring me—but pointing me toward someone who could genuinely help?

I had always seen those responses as a lack of care, but what if they were a quiet form of support?

That was another layer of healing: Realizing that care doesn't always come packaged the way we expect.

Sometimes, growth means letting go of the idea that support must feel a certain way. It means recognizing that being redirected isn't getting pushed away—it's being led forward.

And yes, it's uncomfortable. But the comfort zone is painful for a reason. It keeps us safe but small.

The road beyond it? That's where growth lives. That's where God meets us in more profound ways. And that's where I'm learning to walk—step by step.

Reflection: – Becoming Capable

What's one moment that made you realize you're not the same person you used to be?

There's a change happening in me—but it's subtle.

It's not fireworks or some big emotional breakthrough.

That word—perception—changed everything for me.

Once I began recognizing when old wounds were creeping in, I could pause, acknowledge, and release them.

And for the first time, I did it on my own.

No one had to rescue me.

I was capable.

That's when I knew—I'm not who I used to be.

When something painful hits now, how do you respond differently than before?

I pause. I breathe. I think.

Before, I would spiral—go quiet, withdraw, or emotionally react in a way that wasn't helpful. Now, I try to stay present. I try to respond instead of reacting. It's not perfect—but it's growth.

What role does prayer play in your healing journey?

God must be over everything in my life. That's just how it is. Without Him, I am nothing. Prayer is my anchor. It's where I lay down the things that are too heavy. It's not always about asking for something—it's about being with Him. Healing without God isn't healing at all for me. He's the center of it all.

What still triggers you—and how can you give that space for gentler healing?

Being unloved. Overthinking. Making mistakes. When I mess up, I am my own worst critic. That voice inside can be relentless. But I'm learning to speak to myself with more kindness.

I'm learning to say, "It's okay. You're still growing. And that mistake doesn't define you." Gentle healing starts with that. I'm not fixing everything—just not hating myself for it.

Bonus Journal Prompts (Recognizing change, emotional growth, and responding differently)

1.   What's one sign—big or small—that you've grown emotionally?

It could be a response you gave, a thought you caught, or a situation you handled differently. Celebrate it. It matters.

2.   What truth can you repeat to yourself when the old stories try to return?

Write out a phrase, scripture, or affirmation that feels powerful. Let it be your anchor in moments of doubt.

Chapter 11 – Integration: Becoming One

Healing isn't just about remembering. It's about becoming.

It's not enough to visit the inner child, hold her, and speak kind words. True healing means learning how to live with her and integrate her. I want to rescue the little girl inside me and walk with her into every part of my present life.

This chapter is about becoming one version of myself—not fragmented, not lost in the past, but united.

It's about recognizing that the adult woman I am today and the little girls I once we are not separate. We are all me. We carry the same heart, the same spirit, the same longing to be seen and loved. But now, that love comes from within—and from Christ, who continues to walk with me every step of the way.

Integration is when the fear doesn't run the show anymore. It's when I stop hiding the parts of me that used to feel like too much. It's when I choose to respond instead of reacting. When I decide to listen instead of speaking. When I bring every part of me into the light, nothing must live in the shadows anymore.

And I'll be honest—this part of the journey is hard. I haven't fully gotten there yet. But I'm trying. And I'm learning. That's what matters.

Moments I Wish I Had Responded with More Integration

There are still moments—too many, honestly—when I react instead of responding.

When someone says something that triggers an old wound, I snap. Or I retreat. Or I spiral into old thoughts that whisper, You're not enough.

Sometimes, I can feel my inner child flinch inside me. And in those moments, I wish I could pause long enough to hold her first. To say, "We're safe now. We don't have to fight or hide."

I've had moments I'm not proud of—conversations where I let fear speak instead of love and let hurt lead instead of truth. But lately, something's been shifting.

I've started noticing the space between the trigger and the reaction. It's small—but it's there. And in that space, I'm learning to breathe.

Sometimes, I'll whisper, "Jesus, help me see this." Sometimes, I just close my eyes and place my hand on my heart.

I'm not perfect at it—but I'm more aware now. And that awareness is the beginning of integration. It's when I stop abandoning myself and respond with presence instead of pain.

The Wounds That Still Linger, my most challenging issue right now, is still abandonment and rejection. I feel like the others—shame, anger, fear—I know I will get them down. But these two are deeply woven into me.

Living life with the idea that all I need is me sometimes feels more like an excuse the world uses to justify why people leave or why they don't stay. It's as if learning to stand alone somehow makes it easier for others to walk away—and I'm left in the same place I've always been. Alone.

Honestly, it's one of the most universal and painful struggles for those of us who've experienced emotional wounds: Abandonment and rejection.

And let me be clear—you're not wrong for still carrying these. You're not behind. You're human. And you're facing the core wounds most people spend their lives avoiding. That is strength— even when it feels like weakness.

Let's sit with this truth for a moment: "Living life with the idea that all I need is me" feels like permission for others to leave... and I'm still the one left behind.

This is just honesty—where a deeper layer of healing begins.

It's not about becoming so self-sufficient that people stop mattering. It's about learning that "I am worthy of connection—not because I don't need people, but because I don't need them to prove I have worth."

I was never meant to go through life alone. God didn't create me to be isolated or forgotten. He made me for connection, for love, for relationship.

But here's what's changing now. I'm no longer chasing people who don't see me. I'm learning to stop abandoning myself to keep someone else close. I'm beginning to choose the safe connection—not based on survival.

When Rejection Still Hurts

There are days I still feel like I don't belong. No matter how much I heal or grow, people will always leave. And when that thought settles in my chest, it brings the ache of every goodbye I never wanted.

But here's what I'm learning:

I can feel that ache and still not abandon myself. I can miss someone, but I still know I am whole. I can feel rejected and still be worthy of deep love.

I am not hard to love. I am not too much. I am not the girl who always gets left.

I am the woman learning how to stay.

When Old Thoughts Return Like Storms

Things have been turning around for me lately. Not everything, of course, but a good handful—and I'm genuinely grateful for that. But this morning, I had another one of those moments.

I realized something important about old thought patterns. When you're still healing—still a bit emotionally fragile—it doesn't take much for one of those old thoughts to sneak back in. At first, you might not even notice it. It shows up quietly, almost like an uninvited guest you feel too tired to turn away. But once it's in, it consumes you.

Suddenly, you're believing the thought as if it already happened. You feel it in your body before anything ever becomes real: your heart races, your stomach flips, you get a headache, and this heavy fog of exhaustion sets in. Tears start to fall before you even understand why. Fear creeps in. And before you know it, you're spiraling—ready to give up, wondering, What's the use?

Your body begins reacting to something that hasn't even happened. But to your nervous system, it feels like it already has. That's what old trauma can do. It resurfaces through thoughts and feelings that are so familiar, your body doesn't know the difference between the past and the present.

This morning, I watched that process unfold in real time. But something shifted.

Instead of staying in it, I could step back just enough to see what was happening. I could see the pattern. I recognized the thought wasn't the truth—it was just a memory dressed up as a prediction. And when I shifted my perspective, everything changed. I felt my perception begin to clear. I saw the bigger picture.

That's when I realized this is growth.

The more aware I become of these moments; the more I realized they must not rule me. This was a definite eye-opener! I know it wouldn't be the last. But every time I catch it and pull myself back into the truth of now, I get a little more potent.

"We take captive every thought to make it obedient to Christ." – 2 Corinthians 10:5 isn't just about controlling thoughts; it's about aligning our minds with God.

The "strongholds" Paul talks about are like mental fortresses built from fear, trauma, lies we've believed, or old patterns that keep us stuck. They can be thoughts like "I'm not enough," "I'll never change," or "This pain will never go away. "But as believers, we're called—and empowered—to demolish those strongholds by replacing them with the truth of who God says we are.

"And maybe part of my strength—this ability to rise back up—is something I inherited..."

Reflection: – Becoming One

What parts of you have started to feel more united or "at peace" within yourself?

My past. For so long, it ruled everything—my thoughts, fears, and decisions. Now, I'm constantly aware of how it tries to creep in.

But instead of letting it take over, I notice it. I name it. And I remind myself: That's old pain. That's not my present anymore.

There's peace in knowing I can see it and not let it steer the ship.

How do you remind yourself that you're safe now when you feel triggered?

I pause. I breathe. I bring myself into the present moment.

Sometimes, I place my hand on my chest and say, "We're safe now. It's not like before."

It's not always easy, but I've learned that even a few seconds of presence can change everything.

How is Christ helping you hold the parts of you that once felt broken?

He reminds me through His Word that I was never junk.

I was never too far gone. I was never unworthy.

Christ tells me that every part of me—wounded or whole—is His.

And if He calls me worthy, who am I to say otherwise?

Bonus Journal Prompts (Integration, self-awareness, and faithcentered wholeness)

1.   **What does wholeness mean to you—not perfection, but integration?**

How do you define "whole" in a way that includes your messiness, past, faith, and freedom?

2.   **What helps you remember that Christ is walking with you in your emotional healing?**

Is it a verse, a moment of worship, a symbol, or stillness? What brings you back to His presence?

Chapter 12 – Coming Home to Myself

This isn't the end. This is the beginning of everything I never thought I could have.

Wholeness. Peace. Faith. Identity. Belonging. Not because the world handed it to me—but because I stopped handing my worth over to the world.

In this chapter, I want to speak directly to my inner child. I want to ask the Reader if you've ever felt like your story was too broken to be healed or if you think your story doesn't matter.

It's not. You're not.

This chapter is about my homecoming—not to a place but to a person—to the woman I've become, to the girl I've always been, and to the God who never left me.

Coming home doesn't mean everything will be a bed of roses. It means I've stopped running. It means I've chosen to belong—to myself, to my faith, and to the life God is helping me build from the inside out.

I am not perfect. I still have questions. I still have healing to do. But now I know how to love myself through it. Now I know how to come home again and again.

To peace. To truth. To Him. To me.

There will be days—maybe even after all your work, prayers, and progress—when the pain comes back.

It won't look the same as before.

But it might feel just as heavy.

And in those moments, I remind myself of something simple but life changing. You don't start over—you continue forward.
You don't lose everything you've learned just because you feel low.
You are not back at square one.

Healing isn't linear. It's not a ladder.
It's more like waves, or circles, maybe a little like music.
Sometimes you revisit old notes—but now, you sing them in a new key.

If you're reading this and your heart feels tired.
If you've tried everything you know to try and still feel like you're not "there yet"
Let me tell you— "there" is not a destination.
Home is not found on a map.
It's found in your breath, your stillness, your willingness to return.

To return to truth.

To return to grace.

To return to **you**.

And if you forget again, that's okay.

You're not a failure—you're human.

You're not broken—you're just being reshaped.

Reflection: – (*Coming home, accepting yourself, and living as one whole person*)

What does "coming home to yourself" mean to you now—after everything you've walked through?

Coming home to myself means finally seeing myself with compassion. It means not running from the past, not rushing to fix everything, but just being—present, whole, and loved. It's knowing that the little girl in me has a place to live, thrive, and be safe. And it's knowing that God has been walking me home all along.

What does peace feel like in your body and spirit today? How do you know when it's real?

Peace is quiet. It doesn't demand attention. It's when my breath slows, and my mind stops trying to control everything.

It's when I feel secure even in uncertainty—because I know God is with me. It's real when I don't have to prove anything. I can just rest.

What's one thing you're leaving behind for good? What's something you're taking with you?

I'm leaving behind the belief that I must earn love. I'm taking with me the truth that I am already enough. That God calls me His. And that's all I need.

What new habits or thoughts can help you stay home in yourself when the world tries to pull you away?

Gentle mornings. Prayer. Stillness. Time alone when I need it.

Speaking to myself with kindness instead of judgment. Remembering I don't have to hustle for healing—it's already happening.

What would you say if you could speak one final message to your inner child—the one who waited so long?

I would tell her:

"You made it, baby girl. You're safe now. You're loved. And I'm never leaving again."

Bonus Journal Prompts *(Coming home, lasting peace, and rooted identity)*

1. What do you want your inner child to know now and forever?

Write it like a promise. Something you can come back to again and again.

2. What does it mean to walk in peace—not just visit it?

How can you bring peace to how you speak, work, love, and live? What are you choosing to carry differently now?

3.   What does "coming home" mean to you right now?

4. When life gets heavy again, where do you feel closest to peace?

5. How can you return to that space—mentally, emotionally, or spiritually—today?

Dear Reader,

If you've made it to the end of this book, first, let me say thank you. Thank you for holding space for this story and allowing me to walk beside you for a little while.

Over the last three years, I've made more progress than I ever thought possible. But let me be clear—it didn't happen all at once. It came in layers. My thoughts didn't change overnight. My emotions didn't become more manageable in a week. My healing didn't arrive at a finish line. It came in stages... one surrendered piece at a time.

I believe with all my heart that many people want to change. They want peace. They want to feel whole. But the process of change—the deep, honest work of transformation—is hard. Especially when you've lived a certain way for a long time. Our habits, reactions, and beliefs get rooted in us.

Sometimes, we don't realize how much of our life runs on patterns we never agreed to.

To change, you need more than a wish. You need a desire to live better and a devotion to the process. For me, that process included prayer, stillness, and many nights crying in God's presence and asking Him to show me what I couldn't yet see. It also included talking to my inner child, rewriting the stories I believed about myself, and realizing I no longer had to abandon myself to be accepted.

It meant learning to love myself—not just in theory but in practice. It meant feeding myself better thoughts. It meant seeing myself as worthy of rest. It meant recognizing that God never asked me to be perfect—He asked me to be present. And maybe, most of all it meant learning to see the world through a new lens.

Not as something that owed me healing—but as a place where I could walk out my healing with faith, intention, and love. If you're somewhere on your journey—know this: You're not behind. You're not failing. You're becoming. And that process will never look perfect. But it will always be worth it. Keep praying. Keep pausing. Keep rising—even when you only get one inch off the ground because home isn't a destination. It's a knowing.

And the fact that you're here, reading this, means You're already on your way.

With love and understanding,

Juliane M. Howard

Conclusion

You've walked through some tender places in this book. You've looked back at your past, and you didn't turn away. You've held space for the little one inside you. You've listened. You've prayed. You've felt. And that means you're already doing the most sacred work:

Coming home to yourself. This journey won't always feel neat or easy. Some days will stretch you. Some days will soften you. But now, you have the tools. You have the truth. And most of all, you have Christ walking with you.

Let this be your reminder:

You are not broken.

You are becoming.

And you were always worthy of love.

So keep going.

Keep healing.

Keep choosing yourself.

Keep coming home. Again, and again.

A Letter to My Inner Child

Dear little me,

I see you now. I feel you. I know how long you waited for someone to come for you, and I'm so sorry it took me this long.

You should have never had to carry that pain. You should have never been made to feel like a burden, or a joke, or invisible. You deserved to be loved without condition.

You deserved to be held when you were scared, listened to when you were hurting, and cheered on when growing.

I know what it felt like to hide behind a smile, to try so hard to be "good," and to feel still like it was never enough. I know how you whispered things to yourself that were never true. Things like, "I'm ugly. I'm stupid. I don't matter. Why was I even born?" But those were never your words. Those were wounds speaking.

I'm here now. And I want you to know: You are safe.

You are loved. You are so deeply, wonderfully, beautifully made.

You don't have to try to earn your worth anymore.

You don't have to perform for love or shrink to be accepted.

You can run barefoot in the grass again, laugh, dream, rest, and grow. You get just to be.

I promise never to leave you again. I promise to listen when you're scared. To hold you when the past comes knocking. To remind you of who you are—not who the world said you were. You are not broken. You are not too much. You are not too late. You are a miracle. And we're finally home.

With all my love,

Juliane

A Letter from My Inner Child

Dear Grown-Up, Me,

I've waited a long time to talk to you. For a while, I wasn't sure if you'd ever come back for me. I felt forgotten, like maybe I didn't matter anymore. But when you found and saw me, something inside me lit up. Like I was alive again.

I know it's been hard. I know you've been carrying a lot. And I know sometimes you still feel like you're not enough. But I want you to know — you are more than enough. You are everything I ever needed.

When you hold me now, I feel safe. When you speak kind words to me, I finally believe them. When you pray, I feel peace.

Thank you for giving me a home. Thank you for listening.

Thank you for not abandoning me like others did.

I don't need you to be perfect. I need you to stay. I love you!

Love,

Little Me

My Safe Place Scriptures

Scriptures for Healing & Wholeness

Philippians 4:13 "I can do all things through Christ who strengthens me."

Isaiah 41:10 "Do not fear, for I am with you; do not be dismayed, for I am your God.

I will strengthen and help you and uphold you with my righteous right hand."

Psalm 147:3 "He heals the brokenhearted and binds up their wounds."

Romans 8:28 "And we know that in all things God works for the good of those who love him, who have been called according to his purpose."

2 Corinthians 5:17 "Therefore, if anyone is in Christ, the new creation has come: The old has gone, the new is here!"

Affirmations for the Journey

I am no longer abandoned. I am safe, loved, and held.

I honor my past, but I am not defined by it.

I am allowed to rest, heal, and be fully me.

My voice matters—my issues of the story—my healing matters.

Christ lives in me. I am whole because He is my peace.

I don't have to do this alone—God walks with me.

I am no longer at war with myself. I am coming home.

Heavenly Father,

Thank You for never leaving me—even when I couldn't feel You, when the pain was too loud, and my heart was too heavy.

Thank You for walking with me through the shadows and guiding me into light.

I lay every part of my story at Your feet.

Every tear. Every scar. Every fear. I surrender it all.

Thank You for giving me the strength to rise—not in my power, but in Yours.

You are my Rock, my Refuge, my Redeemer.

Through You, I have found peace where there used to be panic.

Hope, where there used to be despair and truth, where there used to be lies.

I lift my inner girls to You—the little ones who never felt safe.

Cover them in Your love.

Remind them daily that they are chosen, cherished, and never alone.

Help me continue becoming the woman You always knew I could be—A woman who loves deeply. Who stands boldly? Who rises humbly? Let my life be a testimony to Your grace.

Let my healing reflect Your glory. And let every step forward be in alignment with Your will. I give You everything. I trust you with my heart.

And I thank You—for never giving up on me.

In Jesus' name,

Amen.

About the Author

Juliane M. Howard founded Mindset Productions, a purpose-driven content creation company dedicated to healing, hope, and human potential. As a Christian woman, storyteller, and creative visionary, Juliane believes in the power of truth-telling, inner healing, and walking with Christ through every chapter of life.

After years of emotional struggle, abandonment wounds, and the long road to rediscovering her worth, Juliane now shares her story to remind others that healing is not only possible—it's sacred. Through her writing, videography, and heartfelt faith, she encourages others to come home to themselves and find peace in the presence of God.

Juliane lives in Tennessee and has become deeply passionate about holistic living. She believes in embracing a more natural and balanced lifestyle that honors the connection between mind, body, and spirit. After experiencing deep inner healing, she now understands that true transformation begins from the inside out. To her, living in alignment with mind, body, and spirit is the key to a whole and meaningful life.

Juliane is also the creator of Voices of Hope and Healing, a live speaking and storytelling series by her company, Mindset Films. Her mission is to help others find hope through truth, faith, and emotional healing.

"You're not broken—you're just falling into alignment."

– *Juliane M. Howard*